AXIS PARENT GUIDES SERIES

PARENT GUIDE BUNDLES

A PARENT'S GUIDE TO WALKING THROUGH GRIEF

A PARENT'S GUIDE TO

WALKING THROUGH GRIEF

axis

Tyndale House Publishers
Carol Stream, Illinois

Visit Tyndale online at tyndale.com.

Visit Axis online at axis.org.

Tyndale and Tyndale's quill logo are registered trademarks of Tyndale House Ministries.

A Parent's Guide to Walking through Grief

Copyright © 2023 by Axis. All rights reserved.

Cover illustration by Lindsey Bergsma. Copyright © Tyndale House Ministries. All rights reserved.

Designed by Lindsey Bergsma

Scripture quotations are taken from the Holy Bible, *New International Version,*® *NIV*.® Copyright © 1973, 1978, 1984, 2011 by Biblica, Inc.® Used by permission. All rights reserved worldwide.

For information about special discounts for bulk purchases, please contact Tyndale House Publishers at csresponse@tyndale.com, or call 1-855-277-9400.

Library of Congress Cataloging-in-Publication Data

A catalog record for this book is available from the Library of Congress.

ISBN 978-1-4964-6786-7

Printed in the United States of America

29	28	27	26	25	24	23
7	6	5	4	3	2	1

We were even promised sufferings. They were part of the programme. We were even told, "Blessed are they that mourn," and I accepted it. I've got nothing that I hadn't bargained for. Of course it is different when the thing happens to oneself, not to others, and in reality, not in imagination.

C. S. LEWIS, *A GRIEF OBSERVED*

CONTENTS

A LETTER FROM AXIS

Dear Reader,

We're Axis, and since 2007, we've been creating resources to help connect parents, teens, and Jesus in a disconnected world. We're a group of gospel-minded researchers, speakers, and content creators, and we're excited to bring you the best of what we've learned about making meaningful connections with the teens in your life.

This parent's guide is designed to help start a conversation. Our goal is to give you enough knowledge that you're able to ask your teen informed questions about their world. For each guide, we spend weeks reading, researching, and interviewing parents and teens in order to distill everything you need to know about the topic at hand. We encourage you to read the whole thing and then to use the questions we include to get the conversation going with your teen—and then to follow the conversation wherever it leads.

As Douglas Stone, Bruce Patton, and Sheila Heen point out in their book *Difficult Conversations*, "Changes in attitudes and behavior rarely come about because of arguments, facts, and attempts to persuade. How often do *you* change your values and beliefs—or whom you love or what you want in life—based on something someone tells you? And how likely are you to do so when the person who is trying to change you doesn't seem fully aware of the reasons you see things differently in the first place?"[1] For whatever reason, when we believe that others are trying to understand *our* point of view, our defenses usually go down, and we're more willing to listen to *their* point of view. The rising generation is no exception.

So we encourage you to ask questions, to listen, and then to share your heart with your teen. As we often say at Axis, discipleship happens where conversation happens.

Sincerely,
Your friends at Axis

---

[1] Douglas Stone, Bruce Patton, and Sheila Heen, *Difficult Conversations: How to Discuss What Matters Most*, rev. ed. (New York: Penguin Books, 2010), 137.

UNEXPECTED PLACES

LIFE CAN CHANGE IN AN INSTANT. It might start with a phone call confirming a diagnosis, the loss of a family member or friend, or the end of a relationship. In that moment, you know your life will never be the same. And if you've lived much time at all, you know that what comes in the days, months, and weeks after the unexpected is a void. And in that void, we grieve.

Grief is guaranteed in this life. It doesn't matter who we are, where we come from, how much money we have, or what our social status is—none of us is immune. The question is not *if* we will grieve, but *when* and *how*. Even for adults, grief can be tremendously difficult and a real challenge to process in a healthy way. But the realities of grief seem all the more daunting when we're trying to guide our kids through the complex web of emotions and experiences that grief brings.

In this guide, we'll look at grief from many angles and answer some of the most common questions about how to parent a child who is grieving. We'll also discuss the best practices for walking with your kids through grief.

WHAT IS GRIEF?

GRIEF IS ONE of those things that's difficult to define with any sort of precision because everyone's grief looks different. It seems like the more you dig into the web that grief creates, the harder it gets to examine. But we must start somewhere. One of the best definitions comes from the Grief Recovery Method:

> Grief is the feeling of reaching out for someone who's always been there, only to discover when I need [them] one more time, [they're] no longer there.[1]

This definition highlights that grief occurs when we lose something. It could be the loss of any number of things, either tangible or intangible: a loved one, a home, a job, a relationship, good health. For our kids, it could be the loss of a teacher, friends, a stable social group, a scholarship, a pet, the ability to compete in a sport, a vehicle, their phone, access to video games. The list goes on. Losing one thing may cause us to feel a secondary loss at the same time. For example, one might grieve the loss of a job, which could also lead to the loss of stability and routine, creating more grief. The loss of good health, while devastating in and of itself, can also bring with it the loss of freedom and independence.

There's another type of grief that's often difficult to spot but equally significant: the grief of what *could* or *should* have been. This form of grief is exemplified by this statement:

> Grief is the feeling of reaching out
> for someone who has *never* been
> there for me, only to discover
> when I need them one more time,
> they still aren't there for me.[2]

Grief is the feeling
of reaching out for
someone who's always
been there, only to
discover when I need
[them] one more time,
[they're] no longer there.

—RUSSELL FRIEDMAN

With kids, this definition hits home in a ton of different ways. One of the most prominent, concrete examples of it is the moment a child recognizes that an estranged parent hasn't been there for them. This is especially apparent when kids continually reach out for the missing parent, holding on to hope that maybe, just maybe, Mom or Dad will reciprocate, but they are disappointed every time. As they realize their parent was never there for them and never will be, they start to deeply grieve the relationship that should have been and what they missed out on because of that lack.

Social media also exacerbates the could/ should type of grief because it bombards kids with images and notions of what the "good life" looks like. When kids recognize that their lives don't match up with what they see or when they feel they're not as pretty or cool as the influencer popping up in their feed, they may grieve that their life isn't as glamorous, exciting, adventurous, funny, and perfect as the filtered pictures might lead them to believe it should be.

It's important to understand that grief is not an emotion; rather, it's a process. Think of it like a box filled with many emotions that needs to be unpacked. If you think your kid is going through a grieving process of some kind, a great question to ask is, "What's your main emotion right now?" Depending on your child's developmental stage, the response could be anything from a blank stare to a disgruntled shrug. In fact, not knowing what we're feeling when we're grieving is actually a totally normal part of the process.

We tend not to even know where to start because in grief all our emotions are amped up and maxed out. Trying to identify just one emotion when we are grieving can feel like trying to pick out the vocal melody of a worship song at church when the guitar, bass, and drums are all set to the highest volume level. You can see the words on the projector, and you can see that the singer is in fact singing something, but the words are totally washed out by a wall of sound. To hear the melody, we need to get the balance right so the main line can come through.

The Mood Meter app is a great tool to help kids identify and unpack their emotions. Not only does it teach them the vocabulary of emotions, but it also encourages them to write a short sentence describing why they feel the emotion they're feeling. Then it gives pointers on how to healthily move from their current emotion to other emotions on the meter. Over time, they will be able to see which emotions come up the most often and learn how to better identify those emotions. Schools have implemented the Mood Meter as a practical way to encourage kids to identify what they are feeling, and this is a critical skill when walking with our kids through grief.

It's important to understand that grief is not an emotion; rather, it's a process.

WHY ARE WE SO BAD AT DEALING WITH GRIEF?

HAVE YOU EVER NOTICED how much grief throws things out of balance? Life is going along just fine—wake up, go to work, come home, cook dinner, spend time with the family, put the kids to bed, and hope to get a decent amount of sleep to do it all again the next day—but when grief is thrown into the equation, the entire flow of our day is ruined. We're overcome with anger, shock, frustration, and indignation, all of which are very normal grief reactions, but they're not emotions most of us have to deal with on a regular basis. Why? Because most of us living in the US can afford to fill our lives with a mound of distractions, allowing us to ignore our pain. This ability to distract ourselves has created a distinctly American way of dealing with grief.

If I can just not think about it long enough, the logic goes, *maybe it'll just go away.*

And since the five stages of grief (more on those below) are hard and painful, why not try to avoid them? Why not hope that we don't have to confront the loss? So when grief comes, we pack our workdays full of events, phone calls, meetings, and late nights. We fill our calendars with coffee dates, hair appointments, soccer practice, and dinner outings. We download the latest apps, photos, videos, games, and social media platforms. We binge the newest Netflix, Amazon, and Hulu shows. Of course, none of these activities are bad in and of themselves, but when we or our kids use them to avoid or distract ourselves from grief, we do ourselves great harm, whether we realize it or not.

To be fair, there are times when grief avoidance can be helpful. For example, in the days after a death when a person

Most of us living in the US can afford to fill our lives with a mound of distractions, allowing us to ignore our pain. But grief doesn't go away on its own.

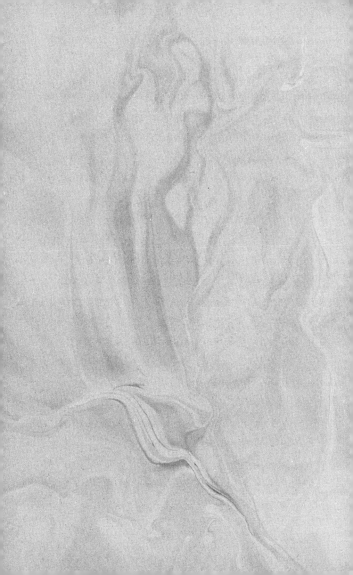

is faced with the logistical nightmare of organizing a funeral, it's normal to be busy with preparations to the point that there isn't time to address painful emotions (that is, until the service is over and the chaos has calmed down). Grief avoidance can also offer a necessary short respite to someone who has been doing the heavy work of digging into their grief. It allows them some time away from the intense emotions before trudging forward once again. Sometimes we just need a funny episode of our favorite show to make us laugh a little bit or an easy, relaxing book that transports us to another world for a time.

Ultimately, though, grief avoidance doesn't work in the long run because the only way to truly deal with grief is to face it head-on, to experience every emotion it brings, no matter how painful.[3] Even if we think we've distracted ourselves or avoided it long enough, we haven't. Grief doesn't go away on its own. Eventually, our pain will catch up with us.

WHAT HAPPENS WHEN WE DON'T DEAL WITH IT?

IN MANY WAYS, we in the twenty-first century have advantages when it comes to grieving that past generations didn't have. We live in a society that is recognizing the importance of mental health more and more—and that neglecting one's mental health can be detrimental in the long term. With this recognition that it's okay to not be okay, we are creating an environment where kids can be more open than before about their struggles, and this helps them experience a more fluid, natural grieving process.

But that doesn't mean our society has a perfectly healthy relationship with grief. There are still many subcultures that discourage healthy processing, and we're all still human, so the temptation to run away from pain will always be there. The problem with doing that, though, is that we can never outrun grief. Grief is not like a piece of clothing we can put on and take off whenever we want; it's like a tattoo that stays with us our whole lives.

The reason for this is how our bodies process grief. Anything that causes grief is a stressor, and stressors trigger specific neurochemical reactions in our brains and bodies, many of which are uncomfortable or frustrating and can cause us to try to numb ourselves in an effort to avoid them. But until we allow our bodies to go through the entire process naturally—that is, until we let ourselves be angry, depressed, lonely, sad, frustrated, etc., possibly for long periods of time—our neurochemistry and brains will be out of whack.

Thanks to these realities, no matter where we go, what we do, or how hard we try to cover up the pain, we can't escape from

Our inability to get away from grief isn't a bad thing—it's actually a grace if we allow it to be—but it means that we have to face it when it comes.

grief.[4] Our inability to get away from grief isn't a bad thing—it's actually a grace if we allow it to be—but it means that we have to face it when it comes. We are giving ourselves a gift by doing so: the gift of long-term emotional health.

If we don't learn to deal with our grief, a number of issues, both emotional and physical, can develop.[5] In addition, people who don't fully confront the pain of their grief can get stuck in patterns of anger and irritability that might not always be apparent. They can look totally fine on the outside, but their grief is still playing in the background. One day, they might explode in an outburst of rage and anger, or they might start having recurring panic attacks. If you're wondering whether you or your kids are dealing with unresolved grief, this article outlines some common tendencies that those who haven't dealt with their loss often experience: https://www.griefrecovery method.com/blog/2015/06/7-signs -youre-experiencing-unresolved-grief.

HOW LONG DOES IT LAST?

THERE ISN'T A SET TIME PERIOD. Grief is one of those things in life that can last for days, months, years, or even a lifetime, depending on the loss and the person who is grieving.[6] Grief is a very personal experience that has no guaranteed expiration date and can come in waves over time, so each person will experience loss in different ways. It can be seasonal, cyclical, or even both, and it can be triggered unexpectedly by memories, events, scents, activities, and images, even many years after the loss.

As we're helping our kids grieve well, this fact becomes extremely important to remember. It's easy to assume that just because a kid looks happy, self-assured, and confident that they are in fact happy, self-assured, and confident. But we all know how deceiving appearances can be and how much our culture tells us to put on a happy face. Don't be surprised if one day your child feels fine and seems to have moved on, and then something as simple as a song on the radio triggers a memory, and they are sent spiraling back into grief. This is all completely normal, and it's important that you are sensitive and attuned to when your child might be triggered back into the grief cycle.

WHAT IS CULTURE TEACHING MY KIDS ABOUT GRIEF?

WHETHER THEY KNOW IT OR NOT, kids are flooded with images and examples of how culture wants them to grieve. Not all the examples they see are negative, though. After a tragedy, one of the most common responses that our kids will see and hear about is a candlelight vigil, like the one held in New Zealand after the mosque shooting.[7] These beautiful and powerful services have become the Western world's way to grieve and honor those lost in horrific events, especially mass shootings.

In recent years, we've seen more and more celebrities opening up about the realities of their lives, especially the grief and loss they face when tragedy does happen. A great example is Instagram star and *Dancing with the Stars* contestant Alexis Ren. Her story is one of tremendous loss: her mother died of cancer shortly after diagnosis. In her grief, Alexis developed an eating disorder, but she realized that how she was dealing with the loss of her mom was destroying her. She eventually found better, healthier ways to honor her mom's memory.[8]

Because grief is so painful, it leaves us wondering, *What can I do to feel better? How can I make this pain subside?* Essentially, what we're asking is, *How can I be happy again?* This is an incredibly powerful question, and if we're unaware that we're asking it, it may lead to destructive avoidance behaviors as we try to cope.

The reason this question carries so much weight in our lives is because our entire culture is built around the concept of what it means to be happy. Marketing campaigns thrive on this question, and

How can I be happy again? This is an incredibly powerful question, and if we're unaware that we're asking it, it may lead to destructive avoidance behaviors as we try to cope.

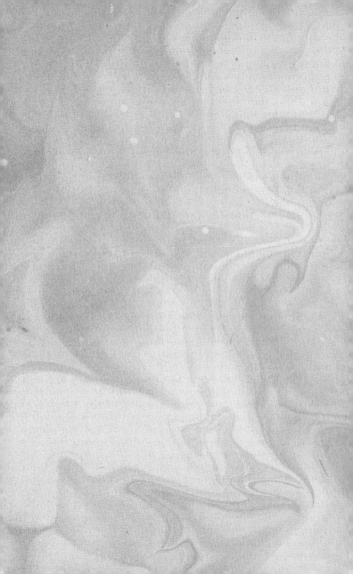

companies will do anything and every-thing to make you and your kids think that buying their product will lead to hap-piness. We've all experienced it: *If only I could look like her,* then *I'd be happy. If only I could have a dad like that,* then *I'd be happy. If only I could have that car,* then *I'd be happy.* If only, if only, if only. And the advertising works, even if we're not aware of it.[9] As a culture, we've come to believe that we must *always* be happy, and that any other emotion is something to run away from as quickly as possible. When we are experiencing grief, pain, and loss, we're bombarded by images of happy people, as well as products that promise to bring us happiness, all re-inforcing the belief that our grief is bad.

In our desperation to regain happiness, we turn to whatever will make us feel good—or at least better than we feel now.

Shopping, drugs, porn, binge-eating, not eating, binge-watching, scrolling, alcohol . . . whatever works. The sad reality is that our kids are some of the most susceptible to falling into methods of coping that can lead to lifelong addictions and struggles.

What it boils down to is this: culture tells your kids that they don't need to grieve, and that all they need to do is chase whatever it is that makes them happy in the moment. Unfortunately, as appealing as it looks and sounds, that's just not how reality works. No matter what the shows, movies, ads, and images depict, life is full of people who know what it's like the next morning when the grief hits harder than before, forcing them deeper and deeper into addiction and the cycle of destruction.

What it boils down to is this: culture tells your kids that they don't need to grieve, and that all they need to do is chase whatever it is that makes them happy in the moment.

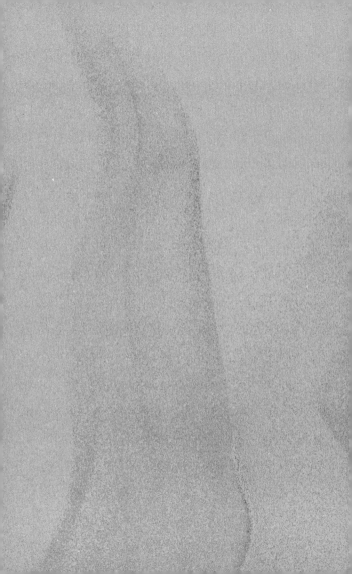

WHAT ARE SOME TYPICAL RESPONSES TO GRIEF?

BECAUSE GRIEF is such a complex and inter-connected web of emotions, experiences, and traumas, a huge spectrum of symptoms can manifest in your kids. Three kids going through the exact same loss—say, moving across the country—can show totally different grief symptoms. One of your kids might cry over everything while another might exhibit relatively few symptoms, depending on their personalities and ages. That's why it's so important to be familiar with the common symptoms of grief. Even subtle symptoms are important to pay attention to and identify.

Take some time to familiarize yourself with the most common symptoms associated with grief (listed in this article: www.betterup.com/blog/symptoms-of -grief). Once you know what to look for, it'll be easier to notice any major changes in your kid's behavior, attitude, or habits. If you start thinking to yourself, *My kid has been acting a bit unusual,* don't ignore that hunch. Press into it, observe your child's behavior, and ask a few good questions to see how they respond when their grief symptoms are addressed.

WHY IS IT IMPORTANT TO TEACH MY KIDS HOW TO GRIEVE?

KIDS WILL DEAL with grief in different ways. For some, opening up about what is going on inside isn't hard. These kids are naturally emotionally aware and can identify what they're feeling and why. But for many other kids, their instinct will be to run from the grief process in order to forget about their pain. Running from grief can take many different forms. If a child who's grieving loves video games, they might get lost for hours in front of the screen; kids who read might drown out the pain by withdrawing to the fictional world of books; and kids who play sports might double down on their efforts to improve in order to focus on something other than their grief. But as we discussed above, avoidance will only lead to negative long-term effects.

Anyone who has ever handed over their car keys to their teenager and gotten in

the passenger seat for the first driving lesson knows how important it is to teach
them the correct skills to drive on their
own. You start them in an empty parking
lot, driving in circles and getting a sense
of how the car moves when the wheel is
turned. Then you help them get a feel for
how hard they need to brake, and you
work a bit on parking. All of this practice,
though, has to eventually lead to practice
out on a real road with signs, stoplights,
and other drivers. Soon enough, you're
on the highway holding your breath as
your teen learns how to merge, hoping
your work pays off.

When we don't teach our kids to grieve
well, it's like giving them car keys without any practice or training. We actually
put them in a very difficult position by
not preparing them for the grieving process. We all know how tempting it can

be to protect our kids from pain and loss, to grieve on their behalf without making them do the work, and to give them an easy out when loss comes their way because we don't want them to hurt. But it's critically important to teach our kids the skills they need to grieve in a healthy way, which means *not* trying to shoulder their pain for them.

The time you spend now investing in your kids' grief education not only sets them up for success later in life when loss comes and you aren't there to walk them through every step of the process, but it also gives you the chance to positively disciple your kids in this area. And the truth is, if you aren't teaching your kids how to grieve, then culture will—and this won't lead to the flourishing and abundant life God desires each of us to have.

The time you spend now investing in your kids' grief education not only sets them up for success later in life when loss comes and you aren't there to walk them through every step of the process, but it also gives you the chance to positively disciple your kids in this area.

WHAT DOES
THE BIBLE SAY
ABOUT GRIEF?

ONE OF THE BEAUTIFUL THINGS about Scripture is how it speaks to the whole range of human experience. Its pages are filled with stories of both joy and pain, peace and sorrow, fear and anticipation—all right next to each other. In Scripture, we get a painfully honest commentary on the realities of this life, and one lesson is painfully clear: grief is a reality.

Nearly everything in between the first two chapters of Genesis and the last two chapters of Revelation deals in some way, shape, or form with a people who grieve. In fact, the theme of grief is woven all throughout the Old and New Testaments. It's hard to find a major character in the Scriptures who doesn't at one time or another break down to show us a beautiful and heart-wrenching example of what it means to cry to the Lord in loss.

Just a few examples: Adam and Eve are banished from the Garden of Eden (Genesis 3:22-24); they lose their son Abel to murder (Genesis 3:23–4:16); Esau loses his birthright (Genesis 25:29-34); Naomi loses her husband and sons (Ruth 1:1-5); Hannah grieves and weeps before the Lord because she's barren (1 Samuel 1:1-16); Job loses everything around him, curses the day he was born, and questions why he didn't perish before birth (Job 3); the mighty king David is humbled to full repentance when he grieves his horrific and abominable sin against Bathsheba (Psalm 51); and nearly all of the major and minor prophets grieve the failures of Israel, suffer for the prophetic witness, and mourn the coming destruction of their nation.

One of the most humbling and striking examples of grief is found in John 11:35.

In their grief, remind your kids that the gospel is big enough to hold their pain and that our God understands what they're going through.

It's the shortest verse in the Bible and simply says, "Jesus wept." The verse is almost haunting. Jesus has just received news that His friend Lazarus has died. Those of us familiar with the passage know that just a few sentences later, Jesus will bring Lazarus back to life, and he will emerge from the tomb a healed and renewed man. With this knowledge, Jesus crying over the death of Lazarus seems a bit strange, but it shows the compassion and deep grief Jesus feels for those He loves. It shows that God feels such pain over our pain that He mourns with us.

God understands our grief because He has felt our pain as fully as we have. Jesus, the incarnate God, experienced hurt, pain, loss, and separation on levels we can only imagine. We don't have a stoic, uncaring God, but a God who sympathizes with our weaknesses in every way (Hebrews 4:15).

Our grief acts as a signpost, pointing our gaze to something greater. In our grief, we are reminded that pain and loss are not how the world is supposed to be. Our grief reminds us that we are utterly unable to fix the problems in the world ourselves, but it also draws our attention to the God who is working to make right all that is wrong around us. That is the gospel story. And even amid grief, the gospel breaks into our pain and reminds us that God is good. In their grief, remind your kids that the gospel is big enough to hold their pain and that our God understands what they're going through. As they suffer, they are never alone. God is with them through everything.

WHAT DOES GRIEVING WELL LOOK LIKE?

THERE'S NO EXACT SCIENCE to tell us what grieving well means for each person, but psychologists have identified five stages of grief that are universal and cross-cultural, meaning everyone goes through them.[10] These stages are denial, anger, bargaining, depression, and acceptance. What's important to remember is that there is no set order to these stages, no set amount of time one will spend in them, nor a guarantee that one will ever reach the final stage (acceptance). So, rather than freaking out if a child seems depressed or angry, we can talk to them about what they're feeling and help them figure out what they need. (Time? Therapy? Space? Community? Love?)

To reach acceptance, someone must have the desire, persistence, patience, and time to work through their feelings.[11] Obviously, if a person doesn't have the desire to confront their feelings, they will never move forward. Persistence is key because, when someone is grieving, they are more easily overwhelmed and often want to remove themselves from the stresses of life. Work or responsibilities at home might take a back seat, and they may spend more time in bed, removed from others. Healthy grief includes time away from the demands of ordinary life, yes, but the person must also be persistent in getting out of bed and taking care of themselves, at least on a basic level. Persistence also means consistently working through grief, both privately and with a professional counselor. We can't simply go to one session of counseling, experience a setback, and conclude that we'll never move past our grief.

Patience is also key. It takes time, and those who grieve well are realistic with

Because we humans often default into thinking we should be in a better place than we are, we all need to have grace spoken over us.

themselves about how long the journey may be. Transformation of our hearts and minds requires hard work, and this is very important to communicate to our kids, who live in an instant culture. For them, everything comes so quickly from all directions that they might feel frustrated when grief recovery takes longer than they think it should. Remember to always encourage them that it is perfectly normal for healing to take a long time and that while the process is arduous and difficult, doing the work to heal from the trauma will have lifelong benefits.[12]

One thing we haven't mentioned yet is *balance*, a central ingredient to mourning well. This means that we can neither deny our grief completely nor live submerged in it 24-7. As mentioned earlier, if we live in denial, our grief will eventually build and cause problems down the road, but on the other hand, if we live totally overtaken by our grief and never learn good coping techniques, we will be trapped in a prison, unable to go on with everyday tasks.[13]

If you have a kid who is stuck in their grief but needs to do some homework or go to sports practice, encourage them to use what's called a containment technique to temporarily detach from grief so that they can focus.[14] In containment, you ask the question, "If your grief were an object, what would it be?" Then encourage your kid to envision the object and make a mental vault to store it. Make sure that the vault is strong enough to hold all the negative emotion so they can leave it there until it's time to engage with the pain again. It might take a couple of tries for them to find the right vault to hold

Transformation of our hearts and minds requires hard work, and this is very important to communicate to our kids, who live in an instant culture.

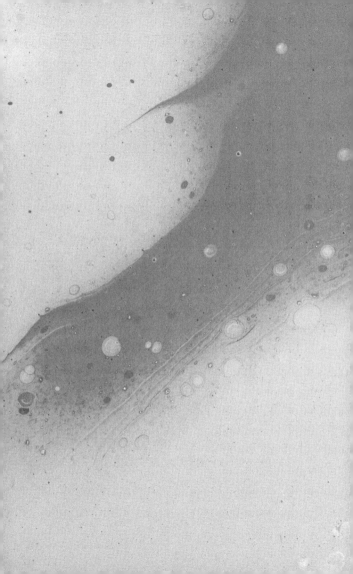

the object, but when they do, a physical sense of relief should come over them, allowing them to temporarily remove themselves from the grief. This can help bring balance and can encourage long-term healthy grief.

As in most areas of our Christian walk, *grace* is a central principle in the grieving process. Begin by giving yourself grace as you grieve. Recognize that what you are going through can take a long time to get through . . . and there are no shortcuts. Be aware anytime you start using the word *should* in reference to your grief process. If phrases like *I should be over this by now*, or *This really shouldn't be bothering me still; I should just suck it up* start popping into your head, take note of that and remember that what you "should" do is give yourself grace.

Kids who are grieving need to hear this grace spoken over them again and again. Because we humans often default into thinking we should be in a better place than we are, we all need to have grace spoken over us. Remind your kids that there is no set date for when the grief will magically go away, but that as a family you are committed to grace. Use this as a teaching moment for how to be gracious toward yourself and to remind your family that the Good News of the gospel is centered in God's abundant love and grace for us.

HOW DO I TEACH MY KIDS TO GRIEVE WELL?

WHILE EACH SITUATION is different, here are three steps you can take to help your kids learn to grieve well.

1. Demonstrate and model what it looks like to grieve.[15] This can be really hard for a lot of parents because we feel like we have to be strong for our kids; we feel like we have to have it all together. While there is wisdom in providing a calm, stable environment in which your kids can grieve, that doesn't mean you have to hide the realities of your own pain. Demonstrating how to grieve well means being vulnerable. It means digging deeply into your own grief, getting help when needed, and letting down the wall that says you need to have it all together to be a good parent.

2. Ask tough questions and answer tough questions. Kids who are grieving tend to shut down from the pain they're experiencing. Learning how to ask them questions that go beyond the typical "How was your day?" can create opportunities for you to encourage them not to run away. This doesn't mean you must ask your kids a never-ending flow of difficult questions. It means you're willing to model what it looks like to ask difficult questions of yourself too, including *What caused me to feel this way?* and *How am I really doing today?*

3. Learn what not to say and get professional Christian help. One of the hardest parts about being a parent of a grieving child is knowing what to say and what not to say. We recommend watching this short video on what not to say when your kids are grieving: https:// www.crossway.org/articles/what-not-to -say-to-a-grieving-person/. However, there will be times when you just don't know what to say, or you might feel that your teen is perceiving everything you're saying as an attack. Because so few of us are licensed counselors, it's always a good idea to get some extra help from a professional who shares your beliefs and can act as a safe, trusted person for your kids to process their grief with. Here's a website that lists professional Christian counselors who can help you through any part of the grieving process: https://www.christiancounselordirectory.com/.

Demonstrating how
to grieve well means
being vulnerable.

RECAP

- Grief can happen anytime we experience loss.

- Grief is not one emotion but rather a mix of many emotions.

- There is no set order or time frame for grief, but experts believe the grief process is made up of five stages.

- It can take years to fully work through our grief, but we must be persistent and patient in our process.

- The Bible is full of examples of people who grieved. Our God sees us in our grief, knows the pain, and is with us in all of it.